YORK NOTES

She Stoops to Conquer

Oliver Goldsmith

Note by Catherine Allison

Longman   York Press

Catherine Allison is hereby identified as author of this work in accordance with Section 77 of the Copyright, Designs and Patents Act 1988

YORK PRESS
322 Old Brompton Road, London SW5 9JH

PEARSON EDUCATION LIMITED
Edinburgh Gate, Harlow,
Essex CM20 2JE, United Kingdom
Associated companies, branches and representatives throughout the world

First published 1999

ISBN 0-582-38199-1

Designed by Vicki Pacey
Illustrated by Peter Edwards
Phototypeset by Gem Graphics, Trenance, Mawgan Porth, Cornwall
Colour reproduction and film output by Spectrum Colour
Produced by Addison Wesley Longman China Limited, Hong Kong

Contents

PREFACE

York Notes are designed to give you a broader perspective on works of literature studied at GCSE and equivalent levels. We have carried out extensive research into the needs of the modern literature student prior to publishing this new edition. Our research showed that no existing series fully met students' requirements. Rather than present a single authoritative approach, we have provided alternative viewpoints, empowering students to reach their own interpretations of the text. York Notes provide a close examination of the work and include biographical and historical background, summaries, glossaries, analyses of characters, themes, structure and language, cultural connections and literary terms.

If you look at the Contents page you will see the structure for the series. However, there's no need to read from the beginning to the end as you would with a novel, play, poem or short story. Use the Notes in the way that suits you. Our aim is to help you with your understanding of the work, not to dictate how you should learn.

York Notes are written by English teachers and examiners, with an expert knowledge of the subject. They show you how to succeed in coursework and examination assignments, guiding you through the text and offering practical advice. Questions and comments will extend, test and reinforce your knowledge. Attractive colour design and illustrations improve clarity and understanding, making these Notes easy to use and handy for quick reference.

York Notes are ideal for:
- Essay writing
- Exam preparation
- Class discussion

The author of these notes is Catherine Allison MA, a senior examiner for A-level English literature and a GCSE moderator. She is currently Head of English in a secondary school and has taught English to Advanced level since 1976.

The text used in these Notes is *She Stoops to Conquer* edited by Trevor Millum in the Longman Literature series.

Health Warning: **This study guide will enhance your understanding, but should not replace the reading of the original text and/or study in class.**

PART ONE

INTRODUCTION

HOW TO STUDY A PLAY

You have bought this book because you wanted to study a play on your own. This may supplement classwork.

- Drama is a special 'kind' of writing (the technical term is 'genre') because it needs a performance in the theatre to arrive at a full interpretation of its meaning. When reading a play you have to imagine how it should be performed; the words alone will not be sufficient. Think of gestures and movements.

- Drama is always about conflict of some sort (it may be below the surface). Identify the conflicts in the play and you will be close to identifying the large ideas or themes which bind all the parts together.

- Make careful notes on themes, characters, plot and any sub-plots of the play.

- Playwrights find non-realistic ways of allowing an audience to see into the minds and motives of their characters. The 'soliloquy', in which a character speaks directly to the audience, is one such device. Does the play you are studying have any such passages?

- Which characters do you like or dislike in the play? Why? Do your sympathies change as you see more of these characters?

- Think of the playwright writing the play. Why were these particular arrangements of events, these particular sets of characters and these particular speeches chosen?

Studying on your own requires self-discipline and a carefully thought-out work plan in order to be effective. Good luck.

His family   Oliver Goldsmith (1728–74), the son of a Protestant clergyman, was born in Pallas, Ballymalion, in the west midlands of Ireland. His father, who may have been the model for *The Vicar of Wakefield* (1766), had difficulty managing money and Goldsmith had to work to pay for his education at Trinity College, Dublin, where a statue of him now decorates the entrance. Obtaining only a pass degree in 1749, he found difficulty obtaining suitable employment and moved to Holland. He had no more success there and later toured Europe earning money playing a flute.

Early writing   Like many writers of this period, Goldsmith began writing essays and prose for publication in magazines. In 1761 he was introduced to the famous Dr Johnson who helped him sell his first novel, *The Vicar of Wakefield*. The publisher John Newbery commissioned Goldsmith to write prefaces and introductions to several books. He completed *The History of England* in 1771 before writing what was to become his most famous work: *She Stoops to Conquer*.

As a poet   Goldsmith's long poem, *The Deserted Village* (1770), established his reputation as a leading writer. This poem, extracts from which are still frequently included in anthologies, now tends to overshadow *The Traveller* which had brought him acclaim, especially from other writers, when it was published in 1764.

As a playwright   Goldsmith's first play, *The Good Natur'd Man* (1768), was performed for ten days which was considered quite a long run. However, it was not as successful as its rivals on the stage and he learnt a lot from this experience when writing *She Stoops To Conquer*, his most popular play, which he completed in three months 'to do something to make people laugh'. Like many authors, Goldsmith often drew from experiences and people he knew and his sister, Mrs Hodson, reported an incident which may have inspired the dominant comic plot of

She Stoops To Conquer (see Context & Setting: Sources).

Final days

Ill and depressed, probably from overwork, Goldsmith died suddenly in April 1774. His friends agreed with him that 'there was no harm in him' and it is likely that some aspects of himself can be seen in Tony Lumpkin. In Lissay, Ireland, where the family lived for a while, a renovated pub was renamed 'The Three Jolly Pigeons' after Tony Lumpkin's favourite inn shortly after Goldsmith's death.

CONTEXT & SETTING

Sources

Apparently, while travelling through Ireland, Goldsmith arrived at the village of Ardagh just before nightfall and asked directions to a good inn. His 'guide', the jester and fencing master, Cornelius Kelly, directed him to the house of Squire Featherstone where he was hospitably entertained and where he enjoyed the company of the daughter of the house, treating her as a common barmaid. He only realised the deception the following morning when he attempted to pay his bill and was told of the joke by the Squire and his family who were old friends of Goldsmith's father. Ardagh House still stands, but is now a convent.

Although some scholars claim that Goldsmith got his plot from a jest in *Quick's Whim*, this book was published twenty years after the first performance of the play. The version offered by Goldsmith's sister is more attractive but it is not just the comic plot that is rich, the variety of literary references in the play reveal the playwright's knowledge.

The play's title

The title not only gives the method by which female success is achieved, but also suggests the play's subject is 'She' rather than 'He', which was unusual for the time. When you have read the play, look at how this title reflects themes, attitudes and aspects of the plot, especially the way our interest is maintained even though the title tells us the outcome of the play.

The subtitle

The subtitle, *The Mistakes of a Night*, reminds us of Shakespeare's *Midsummer Night's Dream* and the play certainly reflects similar concerns of romantic love, using comedy as a way of challenging contemporary ideas of class, life-choices and gender. Underneath the farcical comedy lie social concerns and possible criticisms of Goldsmith's society.

Restoration theatre

The Civil War began in 1642 when the Puritans seized power and King Charles I fled from London. The Puritans closed the theatres, encouraging instead moral and political essays which became the dominant literary forms. Prose writing laid the foundations of the novel which emerged as the most popular literary form in the nineteenth century.

In 1660, with the return of the monarchy and the restoration of Charles II to the throne, the theatres reopened. With their reopening came a new style of comedy (see Literary Terms), now known as 'Restoration' comedy. It was greatly influenced by the French theatre, reflecting aristocratic tastes and the fact that Charles II had spent his years of exile in France. These comedies tended to be concerned with sexual intrigue and innuendo (see Literary Terms) – of cheated husbands and gossiping ladies. The plays did not appeal to the middle classes – not even *The Way of the World* by William Congreve (1670–1729) and *The Recruiting Officer* by George Farquhar (1677–1707). Today, both these plays are regularly performed and are often seen as representative of Restoration comedy.

Sentimental comedy

The 'sentimental comedy' genre (see Literary Terms) which emerged was much more popular. Plays by authors such as Sir Richard Steele (1672–1729) and

Mrs Susannah Centrilivre (1667–1723) were preferred. These dealt with life in moral and sentimental ways, blurring the lines between **tragedy** and **comedy** and often using **melodrama** (see Literary Terms) for effect. Few of these plays are performed or read today, although it has been argued that they were the soap operas of their time. Goldsmith disliked the 'sentimental comedy' with its lack of realism and its emphasis on shallow sympathy. He felt that comedy should demonstrate humour and nature, portraying characters effectively. Although he used some features of sentimental comedy in his play, the strong **satire** and elements of **farce** (see Literary Terms) served to mock them.

The well-made play

She Stoops To Conquer is an example of what has been called the **well-made play** (see Literary Terms). Learning from his audience's reaction to *The Good Natur'd Man*, Goldsmith crafted this play carefully, giving more information about characters and their situations; placing them in a plot which was convincing and almost predictable once the main situation had been established. *She Stoops to Conquer* has **running gags** (see Literary Terms); the recognition of their development giving us enjoyment as we wait for Marlow's squirming embarrassment once he finds out what we already know. It could be argued that in *She Stoops to Conquer* we can see the origin of the late twentieth-century **situation comedy** (see Literary Terms) that forms such a large part of television schedules.

Town and country in eighteenth-century England

To enjoy Goldsmith's jokes fully, it is important to understand that in eighteenth-century England, there was a vast difference between town and country. Any reader of Jane Austen's books (written slightly later) can detect the satire with which she deals with 'polite society', especially in her descriptions of the visits to

Bath and London made by young women from the country. The audience is expected to laugh at Mrs Hardcastle's desire to be part of this 'society', which was probably a wish shared by many ladies living in the country. Mr Hardcastle, however, prefers to ridicule a social situation which he sees as shallow and pretentious. Travel was largely by stagecoach, though the wealthy might have their own horses and carriages, and the fastest rate was sixty miles a day along rutted and unmade roads. Ladies who did not live in fashionable towns had to pay prolonged visits to relatives and friends if they were to join in 'society'. Mrs Hardcastle represents the lady who would like to be fashionable but is not, receiving all her information second-hand from magazines.

Part two

Summaries

General Summary

Act I

The play opens in the home of Mr and Mrs Hardcastle, somewhere in the country. The conversation outlines the relationships between the family which includes Tony Lumpkin, the son of Mrs Hardcastle and step-son of Mr Hardcastle, the couple's daughter Kate and a cousin, Constance Neville, who Mrs Hardcastle would like her son to marry. There is a suggestion that Constance's inheritance of jewellery is a large attraction for Mrs Hardcastle who would like to keep the fortune in the family. The couple are waiting for the arrival of the son of their friend, Sir Charles Marlow, who they hope will marry Kate.

Young Marlow and his friend George Hastings lose their way. Hastings is accompanying Marlow because he is in love with Constance Neville and hopes to have the opportunity to see her again. They chance to stop at Tony Lumpkin's favourite pub, The Three Pigeons alehouse, and ask him directions. The joke is established when he directs them to his own house giving them the impression that it is an inn where they may spend the night.

Acts II and III

Marlow is shy with women of his own class but more relaxed and flirtatious with working-class women, so that when he meets Kate, whom he takes to be the barmaid, he appears confident and assured. He mistakenly takes Mr Hardcastle for the innkeeper and his behaviour as a paying customer offends Mr Hardcastle who obviously knows who Marlow is.

When Hastings meets Constance, he realises the mistake but chooses not to tell Marlow as he sees the opportunity to elope with Constance. When Kate is introduced formally to Marlow as a potential bride, his shyness and clumsiness in her presence is obvious and she decides to continue the trick in order to know him better and see whether she can 'conquer' him. Meanwhile Mr Hardcastle becomes increasingly irritated by the behaviour of his friend's son.

Acts IV and V Various problems arise in arranging the elopement of Constance and Hastings. Tony attempts to help obtain Constance's jewels, carefully hidden by Mrs Hardcastle, as he does not wish to marry Constance. But a note which gives the planned elopement away is intercepted by Mrs Hardcastle who insists on taking Constance to her aunt Pedigree to remove her from Hastings. Tony accompanies them but tricks them into going round and round the grounds, finally landing his mother in the duckpond.

Marlow becomes aware of his mistake and is very embarrassed and ashamed at his behaviour, not least his treatment of Kate who he took to be a poor relation of the family. But Kate's plan has worked. Both Sir Charles Marlow and Mr Hardcastle hear Marlow's declaration of love to Kate and all the errors of mistaken identity are revealed and resolved. Finally the marriage of Constance and Hastings is agreed, Kate and Marlow agree to marry and Tony discovers that he is old enough to have his inheritance and happily looks forward to a future in the alehouse.

DETAILED SUMMARIES

PROLOGUE

In the eighteenth century it was not unusual for a prologue or apologia to be given before the performance of a play. This one was written by David Garrick, the famous actor and manager of the Drury Lane Theatre: perhaps Dr Johnson, Goldsmith's friend, encouraged him to write it. The actor Edward Woodward, who declined a part in the play, performed the original 'dressed in black, and holding a Handkerchief to his Eyes' in mourning for the 'comic muse'.

COMMENT
Goldsmith makes clear his dislike of 'sentimental comedy'.

His argument is that true comedy is dying because of 'sentimental comedy' and that if this form comes to dominate the theatre then he and the other actors in the play will lose their jobs. He quotes, mockingly, a few lines from *The Hind and the Panther*, a poem by the popular John Dryden, and finally makes the point that Goldsmith has come to save comedy. Using the idea of five potions (remedies), corresponding to the five acts of the play, he claims that comedy will be cured.

The argument is an **extended metaphor** (see Literary Terms). **Comedy** (see Literary Terms) is the patient dying of sentimentalism. Goldsmith is the doctor who is trying to cure it and the audience will decide the extent to which he is succeeds. The prologue followed the Greek convention of chorus and commentary and was considered very important. It is a good example of a typical prologue, written in **rhyming couplets** of **iambic pentameters** (see Literary Terms).

GLOSSARY   **comic muse** Thalia, in Greek mythology, the muse of comedy and pastoral poetry. The nine muses, the daughters of Zeus and Mnemosyne, were often regarded as an inspiration for writers

play'r actor

mawkish drab worthless woman; here linked to the writers of sentimental comedy

sententious pompous and moralising

all that is gold ... originally from *The Merchant of Venice*, the phrase refers to appearances and reality and also, here,

to lines from Dryden's poem *The Hind and the Panther*
(1685)
the maid the muse of comedy
regular doctor
quack fake doctor

ACT I

SCENE 1   Mrs Hardcastle is complaining about living in an old
house that looks 'for all the world like an inn' (p. 1), the
provincial nature of the neighbours and not being able
to go to London.

Mr Hardcastle obviously enjoys 'every thing that's old'
(p. 2) and has a completely different view, believing
London society to be 'the follies of the town' (p. 1).
They discuss her son Tony, each having different views
of his character. We see Tony briefly as he leaves for
The Three Pigeons alehouse.

Mr Hardcastle informs their daughter Kate of a
prospective marriage to the son of his friend Sir Charles
Marlow. She is willing to have an arranged marriage if
the man is suitable and to her liking. Constance Neville
enters, hears Kate's news and informs her that her
admirer, Mr Hastings, is the best friend of Mr Marlow.
She is able to give more information about the
prospective suitor. Apparently among women of his
own class, he is reserved, shy and modest, but among
women of the lower classes he is 'a very different
character', something which interests Kate. The two
girls discuss Mrs Hardcastle's plans for Constance to
marry Tony; their dislike of the prospect is apparently
shared by Tony.

COMMENT   Conventionally, a play's first act should give enough
information so that the audience can predict what
is likely to happen. This is a particularly enjoyable
feature of comedy especially when the audience knows

more than any one character in the play. In the first scene Goldsmith gives us the following information:

- The relationship of the characters: Mr and Mrs Hardcastle, her son Tony by a first marriage and their daughter Kate; the situation of Constance Neville.
- The nature of the characters: Mrs Hardcastle's pretensions, Mr Hardcastle's plainness, Kate's wisdom and practicality. Tony is established as a spoilt, drinking, illiterate clod, whose mother intends him to marry Constance.
- The situation: the Hardcastles are preparing for the arrival of the son of Sir Charles Marlow, a family friend. Mr Hardcastle hopes that Kate will find him a suitable husband for he is 'one of the most bashful and reserved young fellows in all the world' (p. 5), a personality which Kate does not find endearing. She finds Constance's information about the other side of his personality far more interesting.

Read the scene closely to note just how Goldsmith provides us with information.

Goldsmith gives plenty of information here and it would be a good exercise to identify what is given concerning character, situation and possible plot. See whether you can work out how the playwright sets the situation up and offers the audience a clue as to what might happen next. The knockabout humour between Tony and his mother, her personality and her husband's fond indulgence of it is also a source of humour. Kate's feisty nature gives us a different view of women from that in the earlier Restoration comedies or in the contemporary sentimental comedies.

GLOSSARY

to town normally refers to London

fopperies affectations

Prince Eugène (1663–1736), Austrian general and ally of the British in wars against the Turks and the French

Duke of Marlborough (1650–1722), British general who defeated the French at the Battle of Blenheim in 1704

trumpery frivolities

Darby ... Joan names normally used to refer to a happy old
couple, first mentioned in a ballad by Henry Woodfall
(1664–1721)

quotha! huh!

exciseman customs man

little Aminadab slang word for a Quaker

muster first day of enlistment; he is saying that his servants are
not well trained in the reception of guests

tête-à-tête French phrase meaning, literally, head to head, used
to refer to conversation between two people

SCENE 2

The scene shows Tony in the company of his rustic
friends. He appears as an amiable young man, who likes
the company of barmaids and who would probably
spend his inheritance in the alehouse. The song he
sings describes his preferences and attitude to life,
making the joke that 'good liquor' (alcohol) brings
forgetfulness just like the Lethe, the river of
forgetfulness. Marlow and Hastings arrive, lost and
looking for directions. After giving a comic description
of a twisted route that would be difficult to follow at
night, Tony directs them to his own house pretending

it is the best inn in the area. To explain the behaviour
of his stepfather he says that the 'landlord' likes to

consider himself a gentleman. The landlord's comment at the end of the scene suggests that Tony has a reputation as a prankster or joker.

COMMENT
Tony plays his joke.

The plot begins here with Tony misdirecting Marlow and Hastings, thus setting up the central joke of mistaken identities. From what we have learnt in Scene 1, we can predict the rest of the plot and the possible consequences of the prank. It is an opportunity to expand Tony's character and the ribald atmosphere is humorous. From this scene, it would be worth jotting down notes about Tony and observing how Goldsmith builds his character through the play to be more than just an immature, silly country boy. His description of his sister and the rest of the family is also a source of amusement and also a possible, if unsympathetic, interpretation of their characters.

It is also worth noting the use of Latin words and **allusions** (see Literary Terms) in the first verse of the song Tony sings, suggesting that he has picked up some learning, despite his lack of literacy.

GLOSSARY

Lethes ... Styxes ... Stygians in Greek mythology the Lethe was the river of forgetfulness, the Styx the river of Hades in the underworld and Stygian is the adjective referring to the river Styx

Quis ... Quaes ... Quods Latin relative pronouns meaning who, which and what

skinful full with drink, literally 'bellyful'

jorum large drinking container, normally used for punch but could also refer to the contents. A modern version could be 'I'll have a glass'

bustard large game bird, now extinct in Britain

widgeons wild duck

nothing that's low reference to the conventions of contemporary drama by using rustic and common people. It is also a sarcastic comment about the criticisms of his first play, *The Good Natur'd Man*

concatenation a chain of events or a thought-process

to dance a bear suggests earning money through supervising a dancing bear, common at fairs in this period, now illegal

Father-in-law Tony uses the phrase literally, for Hardcastle is father by law, i.e. his stepfather

trapesing flaunting

trolloping untidy

blade man of dashing appearance, wearing a sword

A *Identify the speaker.*

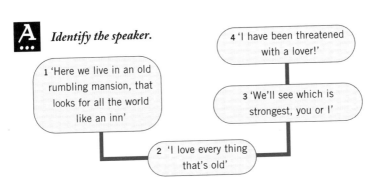

Identify the person 'to whom' this comment refers.

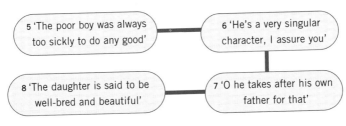

Check your answers on page 75.

B *Consider these issues.*

a The use of a prologue in outlining the author's aims.

b The significance of Mrs Hardcastle's description of the house in establishing the possibility of the practical joke that follows.

c Miss Neville's description of Marlow's character that enables the deception to occur.

d The information given by Goldsmith, through his characters, that lays the foundations for the plot and sub-plot.

e What we are supposed to feel about Tony Lumpkin.

f The effect on the audience at the end of the act, waiting for the practical joke to be played out.

g The comic effect of the characterisation of Mrs Neville.

h The use of rural names and description to create humour and comment on the social situation of the time.

Act II

Scene 1

The town gentlemen reach the inn.

Hardcastle is trying to train his servants in the art of waiting at table. Diggory, the main servant, proves the most difficult to train and the light-hearted banter between them is not only a source of humour but also evidence of characterisation. They abandon Hardcastle once the guests arrive. Hastings and Marlow, believing they have arrived an inn, act as paying customers which disconcerts Mr Hardcastle as he expects them to behave like guests. From this misunderstanding, a certain amount of comedy arises. As Marlow's behaviour deteriorates, we obtain more pleasure predicting the embarrassment that he will feel when he realises the real situation.

Marlow and Hastings discuss the problems Marlow has with women of his own class and his admiration of lower-class women. It confirms what Hardcastle has said and reminds the audience that Kate knows this too. The conversation also explains Hastings's feelings about Constance and that he had her deceased father's permission to marry her.

Hardcastle attempts a conversation with the two men who ignore him as they might a troublesome landlord.

Hardcastle tries to tell his stories about his military service but is ignored and interrupted with requests and criticisms about the menu for supper and the state of the rooms. Marlow goes out with Hardcastle, leaving Hastings alone to meet Constance who explains Tony's joke.

Hastings enters into the joke.

Hastings explains to Constance his plan for their elopement. She is concerned about retrieving her jewels before leaving. They decide to keep Marlow in the dark because in his embarrassment he would insist on leaving before they could elope. When Marlow returns, Hastings explains that both Miss Neville and Miss Hardcastle happen to be staying at the inn.

When Marlow meets Kate, he acts with his normal reserve, unable to look her in the face and finding conversation painful and difficult. When they are left on their own, his stumbling embarrassment determines Kate to 'teach him a little confidence' (p. 29). This explains why when she meets him again in her 'housewife's' dress (p. 4), she allows him to think of her as the barmaid.

Tony and Constance enter arguing as usual. Their behaviour descends into blows, but is interpreted as playful by Mrs Hardcastle who follows them on stage with Hastings. By referring to her age and appearance, Hastings is teasing Mrs Hardcastle who has not the wit to follow his sarcasm and **irony** (see Literary Terms). After chastising Tony for his ingratitude for her long-suffering service to him, Mrs Hardcastle leaves with Constance. When Hastings realises that Tony does not want to marry Constance, he asks for his help with the elopement. Tony is pleased to help and offers to obtain the jewels.

Comment   There is some knock-about clowning here as Hardcastle frantically tries to get his servants organised.

More evidence of his character is also given. The servants obviously like him and are not frightened of him, so we can deduce that he is a good master and not normally difficult to work for, offering some contemporary detail on social life.

There is further social comment on the position of women, particularly those in the lower classes. It could be argued that Marlow's ability to flirt outrageously with lower-class women means that he values them less. At this time female servants were frequently abused by employers and the victims of the desires of the family sons. Although here the tone is light-hearted, social documents of the time paint a less humorous picture.

This scene also sets up the relationship between Constance and Hastings. For everything to end happily, it is important that Hastings had the consent of her dead father and that he loves her, not her fortune. It also explains why Hastings is prepared to continue deceiving his friend. The elopement and the attempt to obtain the jewels form the basis of the comic sub-plot.

GLOSSARY

bauld rustic dialect for 'bold'

pleace rustic dialect for 'place'

cartain rustic dialect for 'certain'

wauns dialect for 'wounds' – shortened form of the oath 'God's wounds'

canna cannot

numskulls people with thick skulls and assumed to be stupid

inflame the reckoning increase the bill, 'reckoning' is often a synonym for 'bill'

college bed maker at Oxford and Cambridge colleges students had servants to make their beds and clean their rooms

bagatelle French phrase used to mean a trifle or petty thing

courted by proxy the custom of having a third person arrange a marriage by informing the couple separately of the merits of the other

duchesses of Drury Lane women of low status, often referring to prostitutes or actresses

ventre d'or French phrase for gold-fronted

mistakes of government comment on the unsuccessful government of Lord North who was Prime Minister (1770–82) and held responsible for the loss of the American colonies

Heyder Ally Sultan of Mysore, south India (1761–82)

Ally Cawn Ali Khan, Nawab of Bengal (1760–4)

Ally Croaker Irishman in a comic song popular at the time

Battle of Belgrade Prince Eugène's defeat of a large Turkish army in 1717

Westminster Hall site of London's law courts until 1882

Joiners' Company probably a reference to one of the City of London's livery companies, or professional associations

Corporation of Bedford an association with a good reputation for eating and drinking

Florentine a baked dish

shaking pudding jelly

taffety cream similar to syllabub – a creamy pudding whipped until stiff

Ranelagh, St James, Tower Wharf the first two were fashionable areas of London, but Hastings is mocking Mrs Hardcastle's knowledge of London as Tower Wharf was considered a place of thieves and low life

Pantheon, Grotto Gardens, the Borough Mrs Hardcastle shows how little she knows of London, mixing areas of quality with the Borough which was very disreputable

Scandalous Magazine possibly referring to *The Town and Country Magazine* which contained gossip and stories about society people

dégagée French for 'casual'

friseur French for 'hairdresser'

inoculation method of preventing smallpox introduced in 1721 from Turkey by Lady Mary Wortley Montague. By the time of the play, it was recognised as a good defence against the various pox diseases. Before this, many people had pockmarked skin as a result of the various infections

samplers small pieces of embroidery usually containing a moral message

crack this could refer to Tony cracking his whip or a lie. It could also be an Anglicisation of the Gaelic 'craq' meaning to 'chatter' or 'banter'

(Measuring) Tony and Constance are standing back to back which is why she complains that he cracks her head

receipt recipe; 'receipt' is still used in America

the compleat huswife manual or handbook for housekeepers, a forerunner of Mrs Beeton, containing recipes, tips and medical advice

Bandbox suggesting that Constance is over made-up

Identify the speaker.

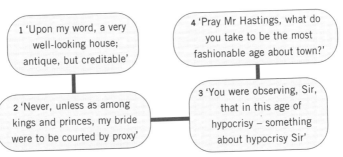

1 'Upon my word, a very well-looking house; antique, but creditable'

4 'Pray Mr Hastings, what do you take to be the most fashionable age about town?'

2 'Never, unless as among kings and princes, my bride were to be courted by proxy'

3 'You were observing, Sir, that in this age of hypocrisy – something about hypocrisy Sir'

Identify the person 'to whom' this comment refers.

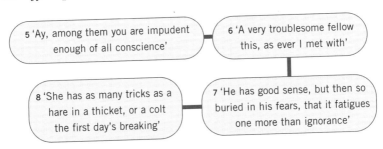

5 'Ay, among them you are impudent enough of all conscience'

6 'A very troublesome fellow this, as ever I met with'

8 'She has as many tricks as a hare in a thicket, or a colt the first day's breaking'

7 'He has good sense, but then so buried in his fears, that it fatigues one more than ignorance'

Check your answers on page 75.

B Consider these issues.

a The comment surrounding social class that lies beneath the humour.

b The portrayal of Hardcastle in comparison with Mrs Hardcastle.

c The ways in which comedy is achieved.

d The structure of the act and the way in which the two plots are furthered.

e The contrast between Marlow's behaviour with Kate as a 'barmaid' and when he meets her as Miss Hardcastle.

f The conversation between Hastings and Mrs Hardcastle and the way in which this draws out both characters.

g The comic relationship between Tony and Constance.

h The character of Tony and whether he is more than just a simple prankster.

ACT III

SCENE 1   Hardcastle is totally confused, unable to understand why his friend's son is so ill-mannered and objectionable. His comment that his daughter will be shocked is amusing as the audience appreciate that she is more likely to be impressed. Kate enters wearing the 'housewife dress' that her father prefers, although unknown to him she is wearing it to confuse Marlow. They discuss their different opinions of Marlow. Kate finds him modest and stumbling while her father finds him immodest and impudent. Obviously they would both prefer the other's experience of him and they leave the stage.

The importance of Constance's jewels.   Tony enters having obtained Constance's jewels by using his key to his mother's bureau and gives them to Hastings who has followed him. Hastings leaves with the jewels predicting Mrs Hardcastle's reaction to their loss. On cue, Mrs Hardcastle enters arguing with Constance about the jewels. She casually suggests that they are only old-fashioned baubles and may well be lost. Tony, not missing an opportunity, suggests that she tell Constance to which Mrs Hardcastle responds that she is only pretending and that Tony should support her. Obviously this sets up the next joke when Mrs Hardcastle actually discovers their loss and considerable humour is obtained from the clowning between Tony and his mother.

The 'man about town' makes his appearance.   Meanwhile, Kate is setting up the situation for Marlow and discovers from the maid that Marlow had caught sight of her and believed her to be a barmaid because of her 'housewife' dress. Kate decides to continue the deception and addresses him as a servant would. When Marlow looks at her face, he is attracted and begins to flirt outrageously, telling Kate all about his activities at the Ladies' Club in London where he is affectionately called Rattle. Interestingly, he gives her a pseudonym – Mr Solomons. After declaring his affection for her beauty and accepting her refusal to show him her embroidery, he leaves the stage as Mr Hardcastle enters. He, who has seen Marlow's behaviour towards Kate, is amazed that she could consider this behaviour 'modest'. Obviously Kate prefers this Marlow to the one to whom she was formally introduced and makes a bargain with her father – that if he sees the modest behaviour she had previously witnessed, he would agree that Marlow might, after all, make a suitable son-in-law.

COMMENT   As in classic drama, the height of the confusion in **comedy** or distress in **tragedy** (see Literary Terms) occurs in Act III and Act IV. Throughout the play, Goldsmith's use of classic conventions creates this **'well-made play'** (see Literary Terms). To ensure the audience has sufficient information, the opening sequence shows Kate and Hardcastle discussing their views of Marlow. The interchange between Tony and his mother is almost like a comic routine with a dame in a pantomime, like Aladdin and Widow Twankey.

Comedy as social comment.

Marlow's attempted seduction of Kate as servant has a sinister side to it. He gives her a false name, presumably so that if he were successful, she would not know his true identity. It is highly suggestive of the situation in which female domestic staff frequently found themselves.

During the scene there are several references which remind the audience of the timescale. It was just before supper when Marlow and Hastings arrived at The Three Pigeons and by the end of the act Kate has promised her father that she will show him the other side of Marlow within the hour.

An interesting activity for this act would be to look at the various ways in which Goldsmith uses comedy. He includes verbal wit, **situation comedy** (see Literary Terms) and clowning in quick succession to maintain the interest of his audience.

GLOSSARY

piece of brass someone who is rude and impertinent

mauvaise honte French for foolish shyness, bashful

Bully Dawson well-known scoundrel who lived in Whitefriars, London

bobs earrings

fibs lies, still used today

bounce of a cracker old-fashioned term suggesting 'I don't care'

paste costume jewellery

marcasite semiprecious mineral that can be polished to resemble more precious materials

your spark a lover, boyfriend

Catherine wheel firework named after the saint, who was martyred on a wheel

The Lion, The Angel etc at this time, large houses often named their various rooms, a practice copied by inns; Kate, of course, is keeping up the pretence that the house is an inn

tablets pad of writing paper; Marlow is writing

nectar in Greek mythology, the drink of the Gods, normally associated with honey

mark of mouth the condition and age of a horse can normally be established by examining its teeth and gums

obstropalous made-up word suggesting obstreperous or noisy

the Ladies' Club group of women who met in Albermarle Street, London, and were frequently joined by men who wanted to hear the gossip

Rattle gossip

nicked seven gambling term

A *Identify the speaker.*

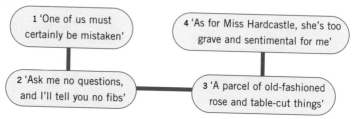

1 'One of us must certainly be mistaken'

4 'As for Miss Hardcastle, she's too grave and sentimental for me'

2 'Ask me no questions, and I'll tell you no fibs'

3 'A parcel of old-fashioned rose and table-cut things'

Identify the person 'to whom' this comment refers.

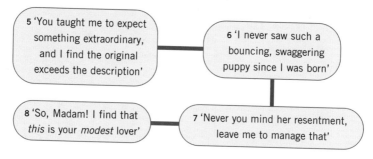

5 'You taught me to expect something extraordinary, and I find the original exceeds the description'

6 'I never saw such a bouncing, swaggering puppy since I was born'

8 'So, Madam! I find that *this* is your *modest* lover'

7 'Never you mind her resentment, leave me to manage that'

Check your answers on page 75.

B *Consider these issues.*

a The way that the different sides of Marlow are shown.

b The relationship between Mr Hardcastle and Kate.

c The way in which Kate controls the continued deception of Marlow to achieve her goals.

d The development of Tony's character and the way in which he helps Constance.

e The various comic devices employed to maintain the pace of the play.

f Consider the social position of women as shown by Marlow's treatment of Kate as barmaid and Constance's position in the Hardcastle family.

g The way the timescale is managed. A lot seems to have happened in an evening!

h The development of the main plot and sub-plot. Sketch out a cause and effect table.

ACT IV

SCENE 1

The scene opens with the sub-plot of Constance Neville and Mr Hastings. Hastings, by repeating the information given to him by Constance, informs the audience that Sir Charles is expected, which spurs the couple to action. After they leave, Marlow enters wondering why Hastings entrusted him with jewels and resolves to leave them in the safekeeping of the 'landlady'. When Hastings re-enters, Marlow tells of his liking for Kate and of his intention to seduce her. Hastings is shocked to realise that the jewels have been given back to Mrs Hardcastle, but is unable to say anything, having deceived his friend all this time.

Mr Hardcastle enters showing confusion with events and also complaining that Marlow's servants have become very drunk. Marlow, believing the house to be an inn, does not understand why Hardcastle would be annoyed, after all he is 'selling' a considerable amount of alcohol. Hardcastle, of course, believes that his hospitality is being abused. As both men lose their

Marlow realises
his mistake.

patience, Hardcastle's reference to Sir Charles enlightens Marlow and he realises, with horror, the mistake he has made. When he asks Kate, she quickly explains that she is a poor relation of the Hardcastle's and that the house is not an inn. As Hastings predicted, Marlow is incredibly embarrassed not only by his treatment of Hardcastle but because of his intentions towards Kate. However, her assurance that she is only a poor relation enables him to maintain his face with her. He also realises that he has lost his heart to her.

As both leave, Tony enters in the middle of a conversation with Constance. They have to pretend to like each other as Mrs Hardcastle enters in order to prevent her from becoming suspicious about the jewels.

Their success is soon ruined by the arrival of Diggory with a letter from Hastings. Tony cannot read and despite Constance's attempts to make up what is in the letter, it finally reaches Mrs Hardcastle's hands and the elopement plot is revealed. Her reaction is to take Constance to her aunt Pedigree, as far away from Hastings as possible.

The act concludes in confusion: Marlow is confronting Hastings with his deception, Hastings is trying to say goodbye to Constance who reminds him that in three years she can marry whom she pleases and Mrs Hardcastle is shrieking. Tony has the last word and resolves to sort out the situation. Bearing in mind his lack of education and his tendency to play practical jokes, the audience are left to consider how the two plots might be resolved in Act V.

COMMENT

*Note how
Goldsmith uses
farce*

This Act is full of the classical features of farce (see Literary Terms). Not only are there mistaken identities and personalities, the muddle with the jewels allows the audience to know more than any of the characters. Structurally, the act, with its many exits and entrances, resembles a farce. As one character leaves, another enters and often the comedy occurs because characters do not meet.

Humour with a long tradition.

The act also contains a good example of traditional clowning in the exchanges between Tony and his mother who uses a device of comedy called **malapropism** (see Literary Terms), after Mrs Malaprop, a character in *The Rivals* by Richard Sheridan (1775), but much used by Shakespeare in his comedies. Just as Elbow in *Measure for Measure* and Dogberry in *Much Ado About Nothing* try to copy their social superiors by using complicated words and getting them wrong, so Mrs Hardcastle informs Constance confidently that she would have her jewels 'incontinently' (p. 57) which means something very different from that which she intended!

Humour is also created in the incident with the letter to Tony. Not only does the audience laugh at Tony's illiteracy, but also at Constance's vain attempts to rescue the arrangement she has with Hastings.

The social comment persists, with Hastings asking Marlow how he could consider robbing such a girl of her honour to be told 'Pshaw! pshaw! We all know the honour of the barmaid of an inn. I don't intend to rob her … there's nothing in this house, I shan't honestly pay for' (p. 49). He compounds his folly by appearing to refer to women of this class as prostitutes but also shows unintentional **irony** (see Literary Terms) in that he certainly will pay for it – with marriage. Hastings also pays for his deception in the loss of the jewels.

This scene has been cleverly constructed to push the sub-plot further towards its climax while maintaining audience interest in the main plot which will also move further. As the act proceeds, so the action speeds up, becoming faster and more comical by the moment as one incident leads into another. The act concludes with Tony stating that he has a solution to the thwarted elopement, leaving the audience in suspense for Act V.

post-coach coach hired to travellers by those who were

responsible for delivering the post to particular establishments. Marlow and Hastings arrived in one and Hastings appears to be using it for his elopement

liberty and Fleet Street here refers to taverns in Fleet Street, London, of which there were over thirty

soused completely immersed; also slang for 'drunk'

Rake's Progress famous set of engravings by William Hogarth (1697–1764) showing the progressive ruin of a young man through drinking and gambling

coxcomb conceited person, normally refers to a foppish man

Dullissimo-Maccaroni young dandies who dressed in foreign styles. In the 1770s they wore red-heeled shoes, cocked hats, close-fitting jackets and wigs, and carried elaborate walking sticks

sensibly here refers to the senses; the modern meaning is 'being responsible' or 'sensible'

I stoop'd to conquer a line from *The Hind and the Panther* by John Dryden

Whistlejacket racehorse owned by Lord Rockingham famous for its successes

haspicolls malapropism (see Comment) for harpsichord

parcel of bobbins wooden bobbins holding thread, often used in lace making

an izzard old term for the letter z

Shake-bag fighting cock; when the play was written such bloodsports were common in England

old Bedlam nickname for St Mary Bethlehem Hospital, Bishopsgate, London, which looked after the mentally ill

baskets sticks

Identify the speaker.

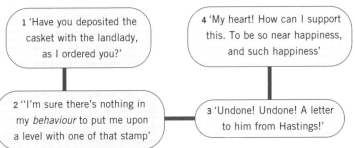

1 'Have you deposited the casket with the landlady, as I ordered you?'

4 'My heart! How can I support this. To be so near happiness, and such happiness'

2 "I'm sure there's nothing in my *behaviour* to put me upon a level with one of that stamp'

3 'Undone! Undone! A letter to him from Hastings!'

Identify the person 'to whom' this comment refers.

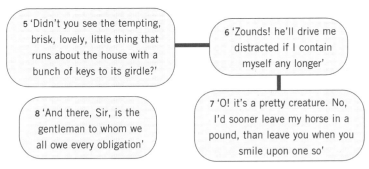

5 'Didn't you see the tempting, brisk, lovely, little thing that runs about the house with a bunch of keys to its girdle?'

6 'Zounds! he'll drive me distracted if I contain myself any longer'

8 'And there, Sir, is the gentleman to whom we all owe every obligation'

7 'O! it's a pretty creature. No, I'd sooner leave my horse in a pound, than leave you when you smile upon one so'

Check your answers on page 75.

 Consider these issues.

a The way in which Marlow begins to change his attitude towards Kate.

b The growing development of the sub-plot and the comic devices surrounding it.

c The clever way in which Goldsmith enables Marlow to discover part of the truth but maintains both plots simultaneously.

d The comic relationship between Tony and Constance and the way in which both their characters are drawn by this.

e The way in which Goldsmith retains audience interest by maintaining the pace of the play.

f Trace the way the 'running gags' have been devised and organised.

ACT V

SCENE 1

Through Hastings, the audience is informed that Mrs Hardcastle has taken Constance away in the post-coach with Tony accompanying them on horseback. The arrival of Sir Charles is announced and the two men discuss young Marlow's mistake with good humour. There is still some difference of opinion as to whether Marlow likes Kate and Marlow's sincere denial that he has behaved improperly with her causes further confusion because, of course, Mr Hardcastle has seen him flirt with his daughter while Sir Charles is aware of Marlow's reticence with ladies of status.

This mistake forms the basis of the misunderstanding between Marlow and Hardcastle when the former comes to apologise for his behaviour. Just as Sir Charles questions Marlow, so Hardcastle questions Kate who acknowledges that she has received offers of love. To try to ascertain which version is accurate, the two men decide to hide while Kate shows them that Marlow does love her.

SCENE 2

As the main plot involving Marlow and Kate comes to a conclusion, so the sub-plot begins to achieve its comic climax. This scene is set at the bottom of the garden and Hastings informs us that Tony has told him to wait there. Tony arrives to tell Hastings and the audience that his plan to thwart his mother has worked. He has taken the coach round and round the grounds for twenty-five miles, exhausting horses and passengers alike, and his mother is now tired, frightened and easily confused. Hastings can now abduct Constance.

A bedraggled Mrs Hardcastle arrives, confirming the details of the journey, and Tony encourages her to think that they are lost, stranded and vulnerable to highwaymen. When he sees Mr Hardcastle approach, he pretends that there is a highwayman coming and tells his mother to hide. Further confusion occurs when, believing her son to be at risk, she throws herself at Mr Hardcastle's feet begging him to spare Tony's life. When she realises the true situation she chases Tony off stage.

Constance and Hastings arrive and discuss the elopement. Constance decides against it, preferring to appeal to Mr Hardcastle.

SCENE 3   The play returns to the main plot. Sir Charles is anxious because if his son has behaved as Kate says then he has lied to his father. If he has not done so, then Sir Charles has lost his prospective daughter-in-law. Kate reassures him that observing her with his son will explain all and so the two men hide. Still thinking she is a poor relation, Marlow makes promises of love but explains that the differences in their situation make a union impossible. However, compelled by his feelings for her, he finally tells her that he will ask his father, whom he trusts, to accept a match with a woman of a lower station than his own.

Sir Charles finds his son's behaviour amazing and interrupts the interview. At this point Marlow becomes aware of Kate's true identity and despite his embarrassment at being fooled, it is clear that there will be a marriage. Loose ends are tied up very quickly with the arrival of Constance, Hastings and Tony. Mr Hardcastle tells Tony that he came of age at least three months ago and that he can marry whoever he chooses. Tony publicly states that he does not want to marry Constance who is free to marry whom she chooses and of course she chooses Hastings. The play ends happily and harmoniously with two imminent marriages and two happy families.

COMMENT   The idea of mistaken identity is continued, despite Marlow knowing that he is in the house of his father's friend. The audience is reminded that Marlow still does not realise that the girl with whom he is falling in love is the girl for whom he is intended. When he met Kate formally, he could not look her in the face so that now he believes that there are *two* women: Kate and the 'poor relation'. This gives rise to further confusion and humour.

The older men spying on the antics of Kate and Marlow is a comic convention frequently used in classical drama. In plays such as *Hamlet* and *The Winter's Tale* it can have tragic consequences. 'Overhearing' like this is a common device in drama. Just as in *Much Ado About Nothing*, overhearing becomes an important device to create misunderstanding and further the plot, so this incident not only creates humour for the audience, but helps the plot come to a rational and realistic conclusion.

The act has three scenes as it has to conclude the sub-plot which begins with Tony's account of his trick on his mother. The use of language, comic names and accounts of duck ponds and 'old lady' (p. 68) to describe Mrs Hardcastle creates humour which resembles stand-up comedy and makes the appearance of the bedraggled woman even funnier, particularly bearing in mind how 'fashion conscious' she is. The next scene is another which resembles classic pantomime, with Mrs Hardcastle as the dame, particularly when she throws herself at her husband's feet. Tony's acknowledgement that she caused his behaviour and character through her spoiling of him, is confirmed by Mr Hardcastle who comments on the 'morality' (p. 71) of the conclusion.

Morality is important in the play. In order not to offend a conservative audience and lose sympathy for Constance, it is important that she decides not to elope but to throw herself upon the mercy of her elders. Her decision to speak to Mr Hardcastle confirms the respectability and wisdom of her character.

Just as Constance has won the audience's sympathy by her appropriate behaviour, so Marlow changes his mind about seduction and using a woman of lower status, showing instead that love is more important. Rather than disobey his father, his decision to ask his father's permission to marry a woman of lower station shows strength of character in both himself and, by his faith in his father's judgement, in Sir Charles as well.

Despite Goldsmith's opinion about 'sentimental comedy', it could be argued that there are elements of this in the final act. The two pairs of lovers are united and about to be married; Tony is happy with his inheritance and The Three Pigeons, and the comic dame has been thwarted comically. It all ends happily.

GLOSSARY   **competence** here it means 'inheritance', the ability to keep himself and his family, rather than its modern meaning of general ability

smoaked for't Tony is explaining that the horses are worn out after going so far at such a pace

slough pot-hole or ditch filled with water

circumbendibus Tony's made-up word for circumference – going round

whining end ... of a modern novel Goldsmith, through Mrs Hardcastle, is making fun of his own ending, likening it to the type of novel popular with women which he often ridiculed

EPILOGUE

This is spoken by Kate whose cleverness got her the husband of her choice. In this speech she takes on the character of the barmaid. She uses the line from Shakespeare's *As You Like It* which prefaces the famous 'Seven ages of man' speech. 'We have our exits and our entrances' and parodies the speech by explaining the five stages of a barmaid's career which link to the five acts of the play.

The five stages are:
- a shy, young country girl starting work
- a confident waitress flirting with the customers
- a competent manager of an acclaimed 'chop-house' (eating place)
- the wife of a local dignitary having succeeded in her life and enjoying cards
- the last stage is left to our own imagination and she requests the approval of the audience for the play.

SECOND EPILOGUE

Here Tony Lumpkin sums up his feelings. It was probably offered because of the character's popularity and a desire to know what happened to him. He explains that he intends to spend his 'thousand pounds a year' and enter society. His last line suggests that he will make an impact on London society, and show them 'what's damn'd genteel'.

COMMENT The epilogue was normally written in simple **rhyming couplets** (see Literary Terms) with a light-hearted tone. Its function was to draw the audience back to the performance and away from the actual plot and was normally a request for approval. If the audience approved they would applaud.

Tony Lumpkin's epilogue was not available for the original performance but was offered later. Apparently, three other epilogues were written but were not acceptable to the actors and the management of Covent Garden where the play was originally performed.

TEST YOURSELF (ACT V)

A Identify the speaker.

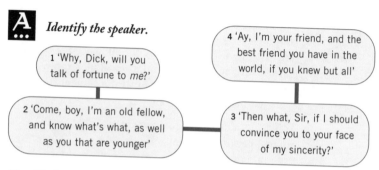

1 'Why, Dick, will you talk of fortune to *me*?'

2 'Come, boy, I'm an old fellow, and know what's what, as well as you that are younger'

3 'Then what, Sir, if I should convince you to your face of my sincerity?'

4 'Ay, I'm your friend, and the best friend you have in the world, if you knew but all'

Identify the person 'to whom' this comment refers.

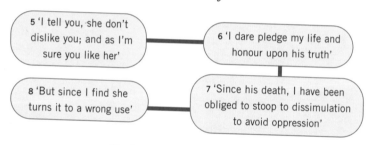

5 'I tell you, she don't dislike you; and as I'm sure you like her'

6 'I dare pledge my life and honour upon his truth'

7 'Since his death, I have been obliged to stoop to dissimulation to avoid oppression'

8 'But since I find she turns it to a wrong use'

Check your answers on page 75.

B Consider these issues.

a The significance of the title in describing how *both* Constance and Kate behave in order to get what they want.

b The way in which the act satisfactorily concludes both plot and sub-plot.

c Consider the features of this act that create a happy ending and leave a good impression of the main characters.

d Look at the character of Tony Lumpkin as outlined in this act. Consider the extent to which 'There's no harm in him' is a justified description of him.

e Look at the nature of the epilogue(s) and consider how justified they are for a modern audience.

f The way in which Goldsmith has shown aspects of society in this Act.

g The balance of power between male and female, youth and age.

h The way in which Goldsmith ensures his audience have something to laugh about right to the end of the play.

PART THREE

COMMENTARY

THEMES

APPEARANCE AND REALITY

The difference between what appears to be real and what actually is real runs through the play; it features in the plot, in the setting and in the **characterisation** (see Literary Terms). In fact, the idea of deception, both comic and potentially tragic, runs throughout the text. Mistaken identity is also a classic plot feature of **farce** (see Literary Terms) and structures the chain of events that make up the play. Although treated comically, each aspect contains social comment and therefore the play can be seen as a social **satire** (see Literary Terms), a play of manners, similar to those written by the twentieth-century playwright, Alan Ayckbourn.

It is difficult to separate plot and character in this play because they are so closely entwined. The plot consists of a series of mistaken identities while characters display aspects of personality that were not previously known.

MAJOR DECEPTIONS

Tony's 'joke'

Tony's direction of Marlow and Hastings to an 'inn' which is really Hardcastle Hall, begins the 'mistakes of the night'. It is a classic prank and typical of Tony's character. It is mischievous rather than malicious and had Marlow been a less assertive guest, he might well have realised his mistake earlier.

Marlow's mistake

Marlow's mistake allows a series of 'jokes' reminiscent of John Cleese's *Fawlty Towers*. The drunken servants would be welcomed by a real inn landlord as the bill would be higher, but obviously extremely unwelcome to a host. Marlow's rudeness to his prospective father-in-law and dismissal of the carefully planned menu is funny but also rather painful.

It is interesting to note the differences in behaviour displayed by Marlow when he thinks he is paying the bill and when he realises he has been given hospitality by someone of equal social standing. Nowadays, Marlow's behaviour would not be acceptable in a well-mannered hotel guest. It is also interesting to see how attitudes have changed since the play was written. No longer is it acceptable to regard someone working in the service industries (in itself a modern concept) as of lower social standing than the customer enjoying the service.

The identities of Kate and Marlow
One of the most important deceptions is that of Kate Hardcastle's identity. Although it is unintentional, her dress and Tony's joke cause Marlow to assume that she is a barmaid in this rather disorganised 'inn'. Marlow is attracted to this 'barmaid' because she is of a lower class and he feels that he can flirt and socialise with her. Although the daughter of his father's friend is the same woman, he fails to recognise her because, being a woman of the same social rank, he is too shy to look her in the face.

To Kate the 'barmaid' he shows a different side of himself: that of 'Rattle', a personality he normally reveals in the company of Mrs Mantrap, Mrs Blackleg and friends in the Ladies' Club. It is this side of him that attracts Kate rather than the bumbling, shy and inarticulate version he displays in the company of respectable women. Kate allows him to continue in his mistake without actually deceiving him because she is fascinated by this alternative personality. In fact, in an interesting parallel, Marlow's activities in the Ladies' Club in London are not dissimilar from Tony

Lumpkin's rural antics in the company of Bett Bouncer. This could be a comment on the behaviour of men regardless of whether they come from the town or country!

Although Kate could be accused of deception, Marlow is no better, pretending his name is Mr Solomons when he thinks he might seduce the 'barmaid'. It is a small detail but shows the way gentlemen treated women from lower social classes. With a false name, once Marlow left the 'inn', the 'barmaid' would be unable to trace him. It is worth looking beneath the humour in this play for possible satirical social comments.

Miss Neville and Mr Hastings

Like all **farces** (see Literary Terms), this play is sprinkled with coincidences and it is a strange one that Marlow should be accompanied by his friend Hastings who happens to be Miss Neville's choice of a husband. Because of Mrs Hardcastle's insistence that Miss Neville marry Tony, Hastings does not inform the family of his position and plans the elopement. The hilarious events with the jewellery, another classic feature of farce, occur because of this deception. Hastings allows Marlow to continue to believe that they are at an inn to give him time to plan his elopement and, as a consequence, Marlow returns the 'treasures' to Mrs Hardcastle, believing her to be the landlady.

Although we are encouraged to sympathise with Hastings and Constance because Tony is not interested in marrying Constance, they have deceived the family with whom she is living. Constance's insistence on appealing to Mr Hardcastle towards the end of the play confirms her integrity of character. The position of parentless young women during this period could be very bleak and many suffered because their guardians were dishonest or less caring than Mr and Mrs Hardcastle.

MINOR DECEPTIONS

Mrs Hardcastle

A joke is made early in the play about Mrs Hardcastle's age. She has been married before and is Tony's mother. She claims to be forty 'Add twenty to twenty' although Mr Hardcastle comments 'twenty added to twenty, makes just fifty and seven' (p. 2). Women's feelings about their age once they have matured have been a standing joke for a very long time but this minor deception is linked to that of Tony's age.

Tony's age

Mrs Hardcastle claims to have been 'but twenty when I was brought to bed of Tony … and he's not come to years of discretion yet' (p. 2). She claims that Tony is not yet twenty-one and therefore cannot claim his inheritance. At the end of the play, this deception comes to light and Tony is informed by Mr Hardcastle that 'you have been of age these three months' (p. 76). Presumably, Mrs Hardcastle is either forty-one which makes Mr Hardcastle's assertion that she is fifty-seven a teasing joke or she lied about being twenty when she gave birth. It is detail such as this which makes this a **well-made play** (see Literary Terms). A small comment at the beginning of the play is actually an important issue that prevents Constance marrying Hastings.

The house

As with Tony's age, the possibility of mistaking the house for an inn is established early in the play when Mrs Hardcastle complains that 'we live in an old rumbling mansion, that looks for all the world like an inn' (p. 1). Her complaints that her husband's conversation focuses on old battles is confirmed in conversation with Hastings and Marlow. Hardcastle's attempts to turn his workmen into house servants causes considerable amusement in Act II.

FASHION AND SOCIETY

Like many comedies, this play comments on fashion and society to provide humour. Modern **plays of manners** (see Literary Terms) still satirise the same sort of people: those who are anxious to be seen to be doing the right thing, mixing with the right company and owning the right sort of possessions. Just as modern plays contain satirical comment, this one does too. The novels of Jane Austen, who was writing some forty years after Goldsmith, also contain satirical comments. If you read *Pride and Prejudice* (1813), you will notice similarities between Mr and Mrs Bennett and Mr and Mrs Hardcastle. In *Northanger Abbey* (1818) the heroine makes a number of mistakes concerning identity and purpose as a result of reading too many fashionable **gothic novels** (see Literary Terms). The society to which Mrs Hardcastle refers and which she aspires to join, is that described in Jane Austen's books.

Dress and appearance

Much fun is made of dress and appearance through Mrs Hardcastle's attempts to be fashionable. This is most evident in her conversations with Hastings who teases her unmercifully in Act II, except that Mrs Hardcastle's ignorance of what is really fashionable protects her from realising this. Of course, Hastings is not just teasing Mrs Hardcastle for fun, his intention is to get Constance's jewels from her: 'No lady begins now to put on jewels 'till she's past forty' (p. 31).

Mr Hardcastle comments on this concern with fashion and society when he complains that visits to town 'bring back vanity and affectation' (p. 1) and again when he greets his daughter, Kate 'What a quantity of superfluous silk has thou got about thee, girl! I could never teach the fools of this age, that the indigent world could be clothed out of the trimmings of the vain' (p. 4). Although many may laugh at the parental despair of the dress of the young and fashionable, there is a serious social comment here too. It also helps to explain how Marlow could mistake Kate's identity as she replies, 'You know our agreement, Sir. You allow me the morning to receive and pay visits, and to dress in my own manner, and in the evening, I put on my housewife's dress to please you' (p. 4).

This also adds to an understanding of Kate's character. She is not unfashionable or unattractive, but equally she is not silly or superficial, appreciating her father's preference.

MARRIAGE

Parental control of marriage is very obvious in the play. Mr Hardcastle informs Kate that 'I expect the young gentleman I have chosen to be your husband from town this very day' (p. 4). She does not object to her father arranging her marriage but does state that she will probably not like him. Although there were obviously parents who took little note of their children's preferences, Mr Hardcastle redeems himself by saying, 'I'll never control your choice'. Although it would appear that parents and men are in control, Kate's determination to get rid of the shyness and modesty that she would not like suggests that women had more control over their partners than perhaps was assumed or admitted; and of course, she does!

Constance Neville's situation reveals more sinister sides to parental control over marriage. Left in the care of Mr and Mrs Hardcastle, she is subject to their permission until she is of age, which will mean a wait of 'two or three years' (p. 7). In her appeal to Mr Hardcastle she argues that since her father's death, she has 'been obliged to stoop to dissimulation to avoid oppression' (p. 76). In *Pride and Prejudice* by Jane

Austen, published in 1813, Charlotte, one of Elizabeth's friends, has to marry Mr Collins, an obviously unprepossessing character, to preserve her economic and social status. Mrs Hardcastle's insistence that Constance and Tony marry is motivated purely by financial reasons, to retain Constance's jewels in the family.

Love and class   Love is shown in the play as conquering all other considerations. Marlow's initial flirting with Kate as a 'barmaid' shows that he probably intended to seduce her, and a modern audience's reaction is likely to differ from that of an eighteenth-century audience, who assumed lower-class women were 'fair game'. However, when he realises that he has mistaken her 'assiduity for assurance and your simplicity for allurement' (p. 54), his attitude changes, and seems to become more honourable. However, this too is linked to social class because if Kate is, as she claims, 'a poor relation' (p. 54) and not a servant, she would not be so easy to discard if he seduced her. Marlow originally asserts 'the difference of our birth, fortune and education, make an honourable connexion impossible' (p. 55) and his character is redeemed by his comment 'and I can never harbour a thought of seducing simplicity that trusted in my honour' (p. 55). Any concern an audience might have felt about his attempts at seducing the 'servant' is dissipated by his assertion that he would never dishonour someone of 'simplicity'.

Love does conquer class differences in the play. Marlow decides that regardless of financial difference, he will marry the 'poor relative'. 'I am now determined to stay, Madam, and I have too good an opinion of my father's discernment, when he sees you, to doubt his approbation' (p. 73).

Inheritance   Although this plays only a small part in the play, it does produce the obstacle to Constance's and Hastings's marriage. Mrs Hardcastle has a mercenary streak and is anxious to retain both Tony's and Constance's inheritances by denying the former's age and marrying him to Constance, thus retaining the jewels in the Hardcastle family. That Hastings denies the importance of Constance's inheritance and insists on eloping even without the jewels, tells the audience that he is not fortune-hunting and genuinely loves her. However, Constance's good sense prevails, as she is aware of how important her inheritance is. The possibility of the difference in financial standing between Marlow and the 'poor relation' Kate suggests it can be regarded as an obstacle to love. However, because this play is a comedy, love wins!

STRUCTURE

Unities of time, place and action

The play has often been used as an example of the **well-made play** (see Literary Terms). In common with the classical structure, the play is divided into five acts and follows the **unities** (see Literary Terms) of time, place and action. The unities featured in classical Greek drama and, together with the five-act structure, were used frequently by **Renaissance** and **Jacobean** (see Literary Terms) dramatists. The events in the play occur in the course of one night – a total of five hours; in one place (with the exception of the inn and the garden) and concern mistaken identity. The action of the sub-plot is dovetailed into the action of the main plot to avoid moving from a central theme of action. As such, the play conforms to the classic structure.

Comic devices

Contemporary critics criticised the play for its series of improbable mistakes. However, modern audiences, used to television **situation comedies** (see Literary Terms), will recognise the use of these comic devices and suspend their disbelief in a way that eighteenth-century audiences perhaps did not. It would be an interesting exercise to compare this play with a modern situation comedy.

Goldsmith's use of stock characters

Many comic plays rely upon stock characters and *She Stoops to Conquer* is no exception. Goldsmith's characters conform to stock types, because the play is a classic one of young lovers attempting to defeat family difficulties that stand in the way of their happiness. The two pairs of lovers are stock types, as are the Hardcastles, representing the older generation. Some of the other characters, such as Tony Lumpkin, have their origins in classical literature. But Goldsmith adds to these 'types' to create life and interest so that **characterisation** (see Literary Terms) becomes plausible.

Continuity

There is a distinct sense of continuity in the play. The possibility of Tony's joke succeeding is established by Mrs Hardcastle when she remarks that the mansion resembles an inn and the deception of Tony about his age is established in the conversation concerning Mrs Hardcastle's age. The confusion surrounding Kate's identity is initiated in the discussion of her dress sense, and her strategy to win herself the husband she chooses is outlined when she declares, 'Yet can't he be cured of his timidity, by being taught to be proud of his wife? Yes, and can't I – But I vow I'm disposing of the husband, before I have secured the lover' (p. 6).

A useful exercise would be to read the play again closely to spot these 'clues' which are essential if the various deceits are to be remotely plausible.

CHARACTERS

KATE HARDCASTLE

Intelligent

Well-mannered

Good-humoured

Independent

Resourceful

Kate provides a balance between an independent, thinking woman and a dutiful daughter. Although she concedes to her father's preferences in clothing for the evening, she establishes her right to choose her fashion during the day when she receives and makes visits. She is also prepared to entertain her father's choice of husband, but it is clear from Mr Hardcastle's comments that she will have the final choice. We often assume that women were in lower positions than men and had little control of their lives, but this was clearly not always the case. From Chaucer's Wife of Bath, to Shakespeare's female characters who kept inns in the tougher parts of London to Jane Austen's heroines, there are more examples of strong, intelligent and resourceful women in literature than there are examples of weak and stupid ones.

Despite Tony's assertion that she is a 'tall, trapesing, trolloping, talkative maypole' (p. 11) we know that this is not a serious character study, merely the remark of a brother. We have already met her in Act I, Scene 1 and she is clearly refined and well-mannered, showing understanding of social etiquette, for after all she had 'lived a year or two in town' (p. 4) according to Mr Hardcastle. Her first impression is of a dutiful daughter as she seems to offer no objections to Mr Hardcastle's marriage plans, but the negotiation about how she dresses suggests that she has the ability to manipulate and compromise to achieve her own objectives.

Obviously she uses this ability in gaining Marlow. From looking at the way in which she controls their meetings, it is obvious that Kate is intelligent and perceptive. She manages to bring out in Marlow a balance of his wit and confidence with his modesty and respect, something which he had previously wished would happen 'This stammer in my address and this aukward prepossessing visage of mine, can never permit me to soar above the reach of a milliner's 'prentice, or one of the duchesses of Drury-lane' (p. 18).

That Marlow finally realises Kate possesses simplicity, honesty, 'courageous innocence, and conscious virtue' (p. 73) is either a description of Kate's character or a comment on how good an actress she is, capturing Marlow with a display of these charms. This ambiguity adds to the play's interest.

TONY LUMKIN

Good-hearted
Prankster
Illiterate
Not stupid
Witty

Tony's name rhymes with 'bumpkin', a word commonly used to refer to rural idiots. That he is a clown is obvious in his behaviour, but his ability to manipulate his mother and set up his jokes proves that he is not an idiot. Tony's character is part of an old tradition: seventeenth-century literature often featured 'boobies', foolish sons, but does not often give them equally foolish and fond mothers; there is a character similar to Tony Lumpkin in *The Lancashire Witches* by Thomas Shadwell (1642–92). The Shepherd in Shakespeare's *The Winter's Tale* combines both astuteness and the clowning aspect of a country bumpkin (and Tony), while Puck in *A Midsummer Night's Dream*, plays a trick to set the action working. Tony Lumpkin's joke on Marlow and Hastings sets the mistakes of the night in motion. His actions are also vital in the sub-plot of the frustrated elopement and it is he who finally thwarts his mother's journey to aunt Pedigree.

Tony also creates identities for other people. Marlow's and Hastings's view of Mr Hardcastle as an inn-keeper has been created for them and they never challenge their initial perception until informed otherwise. Tony 'disguises' Mr Hardcastle as a highwayman to confuse and demoralise his mother. It is because Tony can create these identities that the action proceeds.

It is interesting to consider if Tony is malicious, mischievous or just a good-hearted prankster. His initial deception is motivated by revenge and annoyance. He is angry with Mr Hardcastle for seeing him as a blockhead and in the inn he realises that he 'could be so revenged upon the old grumbletonian' (p. 10). He is not impressed by the patronising tone of the London travellers and gets pleasure from anticipating their embarrassment. The landlord, who clearly knows him well, calls him a 'mischievous son of a whore' (p. 13) when Tony is not listening although, as a paying customer, he is more pleasant to his face.

His assistance in the elopement of Constance and Neville can be seen as either helpful or as acting in self-interest. He clearly does not want to marry Constance and seeing her with someone else would remove the problem. It also offers an opportunity to thwart his mother whose insistence on his weak constitution inhibits his visits to the inn. He may have some suspicions regarding his age and inheritance and is aware that his illiteracy is because she denied him education. He obviously gains pleasure from tipping his mother into the duckpond towards the end of the play and enjoys the spectacle of her at the feet of the 'highwayman'.

Other characters clearly underrate Tony's ability. They refer to him as a country simpleton but in fact he engineers the principal events of the play. He has a cruel wit, and can create situations in which he is able to enjoy the humiliation or discomfort of others while creating a position for himself whereby he can alleviate their problems. But he is no villain. His actions give Kate the opportunity to 'reform' Marlow, for had he not arrived thinking the house was an inn, it is highly possible that Kate would not have seen his potential. Tony also assists Constance and Hastings, both in their planned elopement and in refusing her as a wife at the end of the play.

With a timespan of only one night, it is difficult to establish character development but Tony is more than a caricature. He is initially displayed as a lazy waster and appears to be so at the inn. However, he is also seen by the local rustics as a mirror of his stepfather's country manners and Goldsmith believed that traditional ways produced stability. His drinking and illiteracy are almost a snub to the social expectations of a young man of his class and yet he is not stupid. When he manages to thwart his mother and assist the elopement, he is seen as able to rise above the petty squabbles and arguments that he shows in his relationship with Constance. He makes decisions quickly, is an opportunist and his ability to 'kiss and be friends' (p. 68) shows a benign nature and aspects of a gentleman. He has good humour, is fun-loving and as such is difficult to dislike.

Marlow

Marlow's role is that of the male lover, a stock character. He takes himself seriously, knows what place he should take in society, agrees to an arranged marriage, and when he discovers Kate as barmaid pursues her persistently. However, he differs from the classical model. First, he is easy to fool as Tony and Kate realise and, second, he has a different personality depending upon which woman he addresses. Marlow's role in the play is to be the main victim of deception.

Marlow overreacts to women of his own status. After his introduction to Kate as Miss Hardcastle she exclaims, 'Was there ever such a sober sentimental

Dual-natured
Shy
Confident
A good friend
Boorish

interview? I'm certain he scarce look'd in my face the whole time. Yet the fellow, but for his unaccountable bashfulness, is pretty well too' (p. 29). At this point, Marlow acts as a parody of the hero of sentimental comedy. Yet when talking to Kate as the barmaid, he is certainly confident in his use of the wiles of seduction.

Marlow has many identities depending upon whom he is with. First, when meeting a woman of a similar background to his own, he is a bumbling, bashful, shy man. This characteristic is commented on by Hastings, 'But in the company of women of reputation I never saw such an ideot, such a trembler; you look for all the world as if you wanted an opportunity of stealing out of the room' (p. 17). Marlow suggests that his shy self is his real self because 'An impudent fellow may counterfeit modesty, but I'll be hanged if a modest man can ever counterfeit impudence' (p. 17).

A second identity is that of the confident potential seducer of lower-class women for, as Hastings says, 'among them, you are impudent enough of all conscience' (p. 17) and we witness Marlow's conversations with Kate as barmaid when he is clearly building up to a seduction. When he believes her to be a poor relation of the family, his dishonourable intentions disappear and he is seen in a better light, fighting his feelings for the sake of propriety. The fact that at the end of the play, he submits to these feelings, believing that his father would agree with him, gives his personality a more attractive edge.

George Hastings perceives Marlow as a good and solid friend. Hastings only deceives him in order to give himself time to elope with Constance, but believes that Marlow will forgive him once he appreciates the position. Marlow has brought Hastings with him so he can meet the Hardcastles whom he does not know, make a good impression and begin courting Constance. It is ironic that while Hastings does make a good impression Marlow makes a very bad one.

Hardcastle sees yet another side of Marlow, that of an impudent pup. As far as Marlow is concerned, he is staying at an inn and will pay for doing so, even though a modern audience might consider his behaviour rather assertive. As a guest of free hospitality, as Hardcastle sees it, particularly that of a prospective father-in-law, his impudence is unforgivable. The audience can appreciate Hardcastle's view of him as a boor, as an impatient and ungracious man.

Although Marlow clearly represents the stock portrayal of the traditional romantic hero, it is likely that his father's view of him as a reserved and well-mannered gentleman and Kate's assurance that he has something 'pretty well' (p. 29) with faults that 'will pass off with time, and the virtues that will improve with age' (p. 46) are accurate and that he is finally a character to be admired.

SQUIRE RICHARD HARDCASTLE

There are many examples of men like Mr Hardcastle in eighteenth- and nineteenth-century literature. He is very similar to Mr Bennett in *Pride and Prejudice* by Jane Austen and there are aspects of him which resemble Squire Allworthy in Henry Fielding's *Tom Jones* (1749). Hardcastle represents the things considered worthy and important in English rural life. He has a sense of traditionalism and is conservative; he likes things old 'old friends, old times, old manners, old books, old wine' (p. 2). He is also a figure of mild amusement. His continual retelling of stories of the war is almost a caricature of an ageing English gentleman, and although Marlow and Hastings are behaving

*Traditional
country
gentleman
Old-fashioned
Affectionate
Humorous
Good-natured*

appallingly, we have a certain sympathy for their impatience.

He can see the funny side of his wife and although he teases her, he is clearly fond of her and indulges her whims and fancies, although he disagrees with the way she rears her son. Finally, though sympathetic to her plight when she emerges from the duckpond, his sense of justice prevails and he reminds her that Tony's personality and antics are her creation and he insists that Tony be told his age, knowing that he will reject Constance, so enabling her to marry Hastings.

He has a liberal attitude towards Kate and although he takes the traditional course of arranging her marriage, makes it clear that it will be up to her if it goes ahead. As with his wife, he tolerates her feminine fondness for silk and fashion and has compromised with her about how she dresses in the evening.

He demonstrates considerable patience towards Marlow and Hastings when they behave ungraciously, and it takes some particularly intolerable behaviour before he finally asks them to leave. When he realises their mistake, he is completely forgiving and willing to listen to Charles's father's account of his son's character. Hardcastle is an affable character.

MRS DOROTHY HARDCASTLE

*Affected
Social climber
Pretentious
Greedy
Vain*

Mrs Hardcastle can be seen either as a generally unpleasant character or as a caricature, rather like a pantomime dame. She is vain, greedy and lacks generosity. Her main motivation throughout the play appears to be to keep Constance's jewels. To do this, she pretends that Tony is not of age and that Constance must marry him. When Constance asks to wear one of her own jewels, she is offered a less valuable and less fashionable piece that suits older women rather

than girls of her age. There is little obvious contact between her and Kate and her relationship with Constance is not one of affection. Therefore, it is unlikely that Mrs Hardcastle will create sympathy for her character. She is, however, funny and a focus of amusement.

Her obsession with fashion creates amusement, particularly when she shows her ignorance of it to Hastings who comments, 'From your air and manner, I concluded you had been bred all your life either at Ranelagh, St James's or Tower Wharf' (p. 30). Hastings's reference to Tower Wharf, which was where thieves and fisherwomen resided, is not understood by Mrs Hardcastle who is easily flattered. She is obviously vain and her attempt to disguise her age is an amusing comment on the attitude of many mature women.

Further amusement is created in her relationship with Tony. Her description of him as 'consumptive' (p. 3), as a 'poor boy ... too sickly to do any good' (p. 2) is hardly justified when we hear him '*hallooing behind the Scenes*' (p. 3) and certainly does not fit the boy in the inn. Yet just as she overdoes her fondness, she overdoes her condemnation, referring to him as a 'viper', and 'monster', when he humiliates her.

She is generally perceived as foolish rather than malicious, a figure of fun, a pantomime dame, who should be laughed at rather than condemned. The sight of her pleading to the 'highwayman' for the life of her son creates amusement, but it is clearly her main priority. Her greed for the jewels and her treatment of Constance is foolishness rather than wickedness, and she gets her just desserts in many ways. She is publicly humiliated by being unceremoniously dumped in the duckpond. Her plans for Tony and Constance are thwarted by her husband's announcement and Tony's decision. Earlier, when she read Hastings's letter to

Tony in which he referred to her as a 'hag', she was left in no doubt of her actual reputation.

Her role in the play is clearly that of the **spoiler** (see Literary Terms), but she is also the source of much humour – generally at her own expense.

CONSTANCE NEVILLE

Sensible
Practical
Determined
Affectionate
Spirited

Constance has been left in the care of Mrs Hardcastle and although she is obviously friends with Kate, her relationship with her aunt is not happy. Her father approved of her choice of George Hastings but Mrs Hardcastle is trying to marry her off to Tony. There are not many dimensions to her character although her position may act as social comment about the situation of many women of her time. She has a practical approach, happy to pretend to love Tony when it serves to deceive her aunt and insisting on obtaining the jewels that are her fortune before eloping. She understands the importance of the capital they will provide and is prepared to throw herself upon Mr Hardcastle's mercy rather than elope without either his approval or her jewels.

As in many Shakespearean comedies and **Georgian plays** (see Literary Terms), the heroine (Kate in this play) has a minor companion (Constance). This device allows the heroine to discuss intimate details and plans. Constance, however, is more than just a foil to Kate, she has a well-defined character with motives and purposes. Like her name, she is constant, faithful and level-headed.

GEORGE HASTINGS

Hastings is, like Marlow, a romantic figure but acts as a contrast to his friend. He has a social smoothness and

Socially
accomplished
Not a fortune-
hunter
Faithful
Dignified

an assertiveness that Marlow lacks. He also acts in self interest. His established romance with Constance creates the sub-plot and while he is obviously not a fortune-hunter, he would rather elope penniless than wait for the 'two or three years' (p. 71) until Constance is of age, there are aspects of his character which might appear unsavoury.

He is not averse to deception, indeed he continues to deceive his friend when it will give him more time to plan his elopement. He also teases Mrs Hardcastle mercilessly while pretending to admire her. He flatters both Mr and Mrs Hardcastle and manages not to offend them although he is hardly a better guest than Marlow. He makes a good impression. When he is angry, as he is with Tony Lumpkin, he can be furious but retains his dignity. There is some character development, however, as he accepts Tony's rebuke (p. 68). As Constance is a romantic foil to Kate, so Hastings takes on this role in relation to Marlow.

LANGUAGE AND STYLE

Characters'
language

Although the characters' language appears spontaneous and natural, Goldsmith is using a number of language registers carefully matched to his characters. For example, Hardcastle frequently begins his sentences with 'Ay' and picks up key words in his wife's sentences around which to build his own. Mrs Hardcastle states 'You must allow the boy a little humour' to which Mr Hardcastle retorts 'I'd sooner allow him an horse-pond' (p. 2). He also builds lists for emphasis, such as 'I love every thing that's old: old friends, old times, old manners, old books, old wine ... old wife' (p. 2). Mrs Hardcastle frequently uses **tags** and **aphorisms** (see Literary Terms), often against her husband: 'You may be a Darby, but I'll be no Joan' (p. 2). She also moralises, particularly when she is wrong.

Kate uses two registers, one as Kate Hardcastle, the other as the barmaid/poor relation, to signify the social differences between her two positions. In conversation as Kate Hardcastle, she is formal and her speech to Marlow is highly structured and patterned to contrast with the breakdown in his own (see p. 28):

> MISS HARDCASTLE: I have often been surprised how a man of *sentiment* could ever admire those light airy pleasures, where nothing reaches the heart.
>
> MARLOW: It's —— a disease —— of the mind, Madam. In the variety of tastes there must be some who wanting a relish for —— um —— um —— a —— um
>
> MISS HARDCASTLE: I understand you Sir …

Kate's sentences as a barmaid are terse and quite different, frequently using a rustic phrase to suggest a rural background.

When discussing Marlow with her father she uses a set of clauses and Hardcastle responds almost in antithesis to her. The language the pair use show us the different views of Marlow.

Marlow's broken language when talking with Kate Hardcastle contrasts with the smooth way he talks to the 'barmaid' Kate, showing him to be more at ease socially, and verging on the patronising seducer. When dealing with those he considers his inferiors, he is terse, abrupt, almost rude, as in his conversation with Tony in Act I. When he realises his mistake about the 'inn', his language changes again and he talks to Kate (the poor relation) with a well-constructed formality.

Rustic language is also in evidence, particularly at the beginning of Act II where Hardcastle is preparing his servants for the reception of his expected guests. Tony constantly uses the word 'Ecod' as an exclamation, as well as using many country images. The customers in The Three Pigeons use rustic constructions such as 'If so be that …'.

Allegory

The use of **allegory** (see Literary Terms) is a common device in comedies. Goldsmith uses it for names, to create humour and add to the **characterisation** (see Literary Terms). *Lumpkin* suggests 'bumpkin'; *Hardcastle* suggests something about the character's feelings for his house, while the names of the servants suggest rustic stupidity. The names of the countryside are equally allegorical with those such as *Crack-skull Common*, *Squash-lane* and *Quagmire Marsh*.

PART FOUR

STUDY SKILLS

HOW TO USE QUOTATIONS

One of the secrets of success in writing essays is the way you use quotations. There are five basic principles:

- Put inverted commas at the beginning and end of the quotation
- Write the quotation exactly as it appears in the original
- Do not use a quotation that repeats what you have just written
- Use the quotation so that it fits into your sentence
- Keep the quotation as short as possible

Quotations should be used to develop the line of thought in your essays.

Your comment should not duplicate what is in your quotation. For example:

> Mr Hardcastle is not initially impressed with Marlow:
>
> HARDCASTLE: [*Aside*] Such a brazen dog sure never my eyes beheld.

Far more effective is to write:

> Mr Hardcastle, initially unimpressed with Marlow, considers him to be a 'brazen dog'.

Always lay out the lines as they appear in the text. As this text is not using poetry, this should not be difficult.

However, the most sophisticated way of using the writer's words is to embed them into your sentence:

> Kate 'begins to admire' Marlow when he suggests that their differences 'make an honourable connexion impossible'.

When you use quotations in this way, you are demonstrating the ability to use text as evidence to support your ideas - not simply including words from the original to prove you have read it.

Everyone writes differently. Work through the suggestions given here and adapt the advice to suit your own style and interests. This will improve your essay-writing skills and allow your personal voice to emerge.

The following points indicate in ascending order the skills of essay writing:

- Picking out one or two facts about the story and adding the odd detail
- Writing about the text by retelling the story
- Retelling the story and adding a quotation here and there
- Organising an answer which explains what is happening in the text and giving quotations to support what you write

....

- Writing in such a way as to show that you have thought about the intentions of the writer of the text and that you understand the techniques used
- Writing at some length, giving your viewpoint on the text and commenting by picking out details to support your views
- Looking at the text as a work of art, demonstrating clear critical judgement and explaining to the reader of your essay how the enjoyment of the text is assisted by literary devices, linguistic effects and psychological insights; showing how the text relates to the time when it was written

The dotted line above represents the division between lower and higher level grades. Higher-level performance begins when you start to consider your response as a reader of the text. The highest level is reached when you offer an enthusiastic personal response and show how this piece of literature is a product of its time.

Coursework Essay

Set aside an hour or so at the start of your work to plan what you have to do.

- List all the points you feel are needed to cover the task. Collect page references of information and quotations that will support what you have to say. A helpful tool is the highlighter pen: this saves painstaking copying and enables you to target precisely what you want to use.
- Focus on what you consider to be the main points of the essay. Try to sum up your argument in a single sentence, which could be the closing sentence of your essay. Depending on the essay title, it could be a statement about a character: Despite appearing to be a mischievous clown, eventually Tony's ability to 'kiss and make friends' shows him to be more of a gentleman than previously considered. His quick thinking saves Constance's and Hastings's plans from failing completely; an opinion about setting: The country setting of the play, the yokels and rustic servants add to the likelihood that the deception, once made, can be maintained. Furthermore, the play takes place after dark in the days before gas or electric lighting; or a judgement on a theme: The theme of young love overcoming all the obstacles put in its way is a common one. Goldsmith creates humour from this well-worn situation, ensuring the happy ending traditional in comedies.
- Make a short essay plan. Use the first paragraph to introduce the argument you wish to make. In the following paragraphs develop this argument with details, examples and other possible points of view. Sum up your argument in the last paragraph. Check you have answered the question.
- Write the essay, remembering all the time the central point you are making.
- On completion, go back over what you have written to eliminate careless errors and improve expression.

Read it aloud to yourself, or, if you are feeling more confident, to a relative or friend.

If you can, try to type your essay, using a word processor. This will allow you to correct and improve your writing without spoiling its appearance.

Examination *essay*

The essay written in an examination often carries more marks than the coursework essay even though it is written under considerable time pressure.

In the revision period build up notes on various aspects of the text you are using. Fortunately, in acquiring this set of York Notes on *She Stoops to Conquer*, you have made a prudent beginning! York Notes are set out to give you vital information and help you to construct your personal overview of the text.

Make notes with appropriate quotations about the key issues of the set text. Go into the examination knowing your text and having a clear set of opinions about it.

In most English Literature examinations you can take in copies of your set books. This in an enormous advantage although it may lull you into a false sense of security. Beware! There is simply not enough time in an examination to read the book from scratch.

In the *examination*

- Read the question paper carefully and remind yourself what you have to do.
- Look at the questions on your set texts to select the one that most interests you and mentally work out the points you wish to stress.
- Remind yourself of the time available and how you are going to use it.
- Briefly map out a short plan in note form that will keep your writing on track and illustrate the key argument you want to make.
- Then set about writing it.
- When you have finished, check through to eliminate errors.

To summarise,
these are the
keys to success:

- Know the text
- Have a clear understanding of and opinions on the storyline, characters, setting, themes and writer's concerns
- Select the right material
- Plan and write a clear response, continually bearing the question in mind

Sample essay plan

A typical essay question on *She Stoops to Conquer* is followed by a sample essay plan in note form. This does not present the only answer to the question, merely one answer. Do not be afraid to include your own ideas and leave out some of those in this sample! Remember that quotations are essential to prove and illustrate the points you make.

How important is disguise and mistaken identity in *She Stoops to Conquer*?

As it could be argued that disguise and mistaken identity are the main issues guiding the plot, this will be an extensive question requiring an exploration of the whole play. You may wish to consider how these aspects also provide characterisation, social comment and irony. An outline of the answer might look like this:

Part 1

A brief explanation of the 'natural disguises' taken by the characters in the play. These might include Marlow's different personalities as reflected in the way he speaks to the other characters. You may wish to include a brief discussion of the way in which Mrs Hardcastle likes to present herself and how she really is. You could also include the way she deceives Tony about his age.

Part 2

Look at Tony's deception of Marlow and Hastings and discuss the way in which they mistake the identity

CHARACTERS

Late husband of

Mrs. Hardcastle

Mr. Hardcastle

Sir Charles Marlow, his friend

Tony Lumpkin, their son

Mrs. H. wishes the two to marry

Kate Hardcastle, their daughter

Young Marlow, Sir Charles's son

Miss Neville, the Ward of Mrs. H.

Hastings, his friend

of Mr and Mrs Hardcastle and their home. Look at the way this drives the plot, creates humour and suggests a strategy to Kate. Consider how Hastings maintains the deception in order to help his elopement plans. Consider the morality of his motives.

Part 3 Look at the elopement itself, the farce with the 'theft' of the jewels and finally the way Tony Lumpkin deceives his mother into thinking they have travelled a long way only to end up in the duckpond at the end of the garden. Is this her just desserts? Is it right that Hastings and Constance be helped in this way? You may like to consider whether they are rewarded because Constance makes the right decision to tell the truth and ask Mr Hardcastle for help.

Part 4 Look at the various constructions of Marlow's identity. Who is deceiving whom? Was it finally in his own interests that Kate saw both sides of him and presented them to both his father and prospective father-in-law? At this point, you may wish to discuss the social implications of Marlow's behaviour and the possible irony created.

Part 5 Draw some conclusions and return to the question. Obviously without mistaken identity and deception, there would be no play, but these elements also add to characterisation, tone and create a more serious element than might be noticed in a first reading.

FURTHER QUESTIONS

Make a plan as shown above and attempt these questions:

1 Is Tony Lumpkin a hero or a villain?
2 Mr Hardcastle, Kate and Sir Charles Marlow all have different views of Marlow. Which one do you think is the most accurate?

3 How far would you agree that *She Stoops to Conquer* is a farce with no depth?

4 In your opinion, what function do the minor characters play in *She Stoops to Conquer*?

5 How far would you agree that Kate and Constance are 'silly women'?

6 Explain how Goldsmith conveys his views of fashion in the play.

7 What part does conflict play in *She Stoops to Conquer*?

8 Clowning and mistakes are the main features of *She Stoops to Conquer*. How far do you agree with this statement?

9 How far would you agree that much of the play's humour originates in the misfortunes of others?

10 How far do you sympathise with Marlow?

CULTURAL CONNECTIONS

BROADER PERSPECTIVES

She Stoops to Conquer is still performed, particularly by repertory groups and in local theatres. More common, however, are performances of *The School for Scandal* and *The Rivals* by Richard Sheridan, two major plays from the period which are useful to compare with Goldsmith's play. Goldsmith's novel *The Vicar of Wakefield* (1766) gives insight into the author's appreciation of rural values and way of life.

Although somewhat later, the novels of Jane Austen are useful background reading to understand the social context of the time. *Pride and Prejudice* and *Emma* are both useful in describing family life, marriage and courtship. Both novels contain elements of mistaken identity, but not to such a farcical extent as Goldsmith's play.

More modern texts which might prove useful are *Hobson's Choice* by Harold Brighouse and *The Importance of Being Earnest* by Oscar Wilde. If we consider Goldsmith as a social commentator, you might wish to watch some of Alan Ayckbourn's plays which are considered modern satires on middle-class manners.

allegory where the apparent meaning of the characters and events is used to symbolise a moral or spiritual meaning

allusion reference briefly recalling something in another text

aphorism short pithy saying expressing a general truth

characterisation process of developing a character in fiction

comedy a drama intended primarily to entertain and which ends happily

extended metaphor a metaphor extended over a passage of writing

farce type of comedy that exploits improbable situations

genre term for a kind or type of literature, e.g. a play, short story or romantic novel

Georgian plays plays written in the reign of King George II (1727–60)

gothic novels books belonging to the gothic genre, characterised by dark, gloomy settings, melodramatic characterisation and action and supernatural subjects. The gothic genre began in the late eighteenth century

iambic pentameter pattern in the rhythm of speech. Normally consists of ten syllables to a line of poetry which have an alternate pattern of stress/unstress; often described as *de dum de dum de dum de dum de dum*. A pair of syllables is known as a foot and pentameter becomes translated literally as 'a measure of five'

innuendo subtle reference, usually derogatory, often of a sexual nature

irony saying one thing but meaning something else

Jacobean the era of James I who came to the English throne in 1603

malapropism incorrect use of a long or complicated word to create humour, named after Mrs Malaprop in *The Rivals* by Richard Sheridan

melodrama drama, often romantic, which sensationalises or is characterised by extravagant action and emotion

metaphor description of one thing in terms of something else

plays of manners plays which focus on behaviour and mannerisms; they are often satirical

realism style which attempts to portray issues and people realistically

Renaissance the great revival of art, literature and learning which took place in Europe during the fourteenth, fifteenth and sixteenth centuries

rhyming couplet pair of lines that rhyme

running gag a joke that runs through part or all of a text

satire attempt to ridicule a person or a section of society by pointing out the foolishness or absurdity of mannerism, custom or trait; it is always critical

situation comedy (sitcom) normally refers to a half-hour programme on television where humour is obtained from the situation in which characters find themselves

spoiler term referring to a statement or action intended to undermine someone else's speech or action

stock characters characters which are only two-dimensional and tend to fit stereotypes; frequently used in satires

sub-plot minor plot which runs alongside the main plot

tag a brief quotation or an add-on word

tone general aspect, quality or style

tragedy a drama which traces the career and downfall of an individual

unities in classical Greek drama it was conventional to follow the three unities of time, place and action. This meant that the action had to take place in the same place, within a given time and be concerned with a central heme

well-made play phrase used to describe a play that follows the unities, develops believable characters who use speech effectively, and has a well-constructed plot

TEST ANSWERS

TEST YOURSELF (Act I)

A 1 Mrs Hardcastle *(1, page 1)*
2 Mr Hardcastle *(1, page 2)*
3 Tony Lumpkin *(1, page 4)*
4 Kate Hardcastle *(1, page 6)*
5 Tony Lumpkin *(1, page 2)*
6 Marlow *(1, page 6)*
7 Tony Lumpkin *(2, page 9)*
8 Kate Hardcastle *(2, page 11)*

TEST YOURSELF (Act II)

A 1 Hastings *(1, page 16)*
2 Marlow *(1, page 17)*
3 Kate Hardcastle *(1, page 28)*
4 Mrs Hardcastle *(1, page 31)*
5 Marlow *(1, page 17)*
6 Hardcastle *(1, page 23)*
7 Marlow *(1, page 29)*
8 Constance Neville *(1, page 33)*

TEST YOURSELF (Act III)

A 1 Kate *(1, page 36)*
2 Tony Lumpkin *(1, page 38)*
3 Mrs Hardcastle *(1, page 39)*
4 Marlow *(1, page 43)*

5 Marlow *(1, page 35)*
6 Marlow *(1, page 36)*
7 Mrs Hardcastle *(1, page 38)*
8 Marlow *(1, page 46)*

TEST YOURSELF (Act IV)

A 1 Marlow *(1, page 48)*
2 Kate *(1, page 54)*
3 Constance *(1, page 57)*
4 Hastings *(1, page 62)*
5 Kate *(1, page 49)*
6 Marlow *(1, page 52)*
7 Constance Neville *(1, page 56)*
8 Tony *(1, page 60)*

TEST YOURSELF (Act V)

A 1 Sir Charles Marlow *(1, page 63)*
2 Mr Hardcastle *(1, page 64)*
3 Kate Hardcastle *(1, page 66)*
4 Tony Lumpkin *(2, page 67)*
5 Kate Hardcastle *(1, page 65)*
6 Marlow *(1, page 65)*
7 The late Mr Neville *(3, page 76)*
8 Mrs Hardcastle *(3, page 76)*

OTHER TITLES

GCSE and equivalent levels (£3.50 each)

Maya Angelou
I Know Why the Caged Bird Sings

Jane Austen
Pride and Prejudice

Alan Ayckbourn
Absent Friends

Elizabeth Barrett Browning
Selected Poems

Robert Bolt
A Man for All Seasons

Harold Brighouse
Hobson's Choice

Charlotte Brontë
Jane Eyre

Emily Brontë
Wuthering Heights

Shelagh Delaney
A Taste of Honey

Charles Dickens
David Copperfield

Charles Dickens
Great Expectations

Charles Dickens
Hard Times

Charles Dickens
Oliver Twist

Roddy Doyle
Paddy Clarke Ha Ha Ha

George Eliot
Silas Marner

George Eliot
The Mill on the Floss

William Golding
Lord of the Flies

Oliver Goldsmith
She Stoops To Conquer

Willis Hall
The Long and the Short and the Tall

Thomas Hardy
Far from the Madding Crowd

Thomas Hardy
The Mayor of Casterbridge

Thomas Hardy
Tess of the d'Urbervilles

Thomas Hardy
The Withered Arm and other Wessex Tales

L.P. Hartley
The Go-Between

Seamus Heaney
Selected Poems

Susan Hill
I'm the King of the Castle

Barry Hines
A Kestrel for a Knave

Louise Lawrence
Children of the Dust

Harper Lee
To Kill a Mockingbird

Laurie Lee
Cider with Rosie

Arthur Miller
The Crucible

Arthur Miller
A View from the Bridge

Robert O'Brien
Z for Zachariah

Frank O'Connor
My Oedipus Complex and other stories

George Orwell
Animal Farm

J.B. Priestley
An Inspector Calls

Willy Russell
Educating Rita

Willy Russell
Our Day Out

J.D. Salinger
The Catcher in the Rye

William Shakespeare
Henry IV Part 1

William Shakespeare
Henry V

William Shakespeare
Julius Caesar

William Shakespeare
Macbeth

William Shakespeare
The Merchant of Venice

William Shakespeare
A Midsummer Night's Dream

William Shakespeare
Much Ado About Nothing

William Shakespeare
Romeo and Juliet

William Shakespeare
The Tempest

William Shakespeare
Twelfth Night

George Bernard Shaw
Pygmalion

Mary Shelley
Frankenstein

R.C. Sherriff
Journey's End

Rukshana Smith
Salt on the snow

John Steinbeck
Of Mice and Men

Robert Louis Stevenson
Dr Jekyll and Mr Hyde

Jonathan Swift
Gulliver's Travels

Robert Swindells
Daz 4 Zoe

Mildred D. Taylor
Roll of Thunder, Hear My Cry

Mark Twain
Huckleberry Finn

James Watson
Talking in Whispers

William Wordsworth
Selected Poems

A Choice of Poets

Mystery Stories of the Nineteenth Century including The Signalman

Nineteenth Century Short Stories

Poetry of the First World War

Six Women Poets

York Notes Advanced (£3.99 each)

Margaret Atwood
The Handmaid's Tale

Jane Austen
Mansfield Park

Jane Austen
Persuasion

Jane Austen
Pride and Prejudice

Alan Bennett
Talking Heads

William Blake
Songs of Innocence and of Experience

Charlotte Brontë
Jane Eyre

Emily Brontë
Wuthering Heights

Geoffrey Chaucer
The Franklin's Tale

Geoffrey Chaucer
General Prologue to the Canterbury Tales

Geoffrey Chaucer
The Wife of Bath's Prologue and Tale

Joseph Conrad
Heart of Darkness

Charles Dickens
Great Expectations

John Donne
Selected Poems

George Eliot
The Mill on the Floss

F. Scott Fitzgerald
The Great Gatsby

E.M. Forster
A Passage to India

Brian Friel
Translations

Thomas Hardy
The Mayor of Casterbridge

Thomas Hardy
Tess of the d'Urbervilles

Seamus Heaney
Selected Poems from Opened Ground

Nathaniel Hawthorne
The Scarlet Letter

James Joyce
Dubliners

John Keats
Selected Poems

Christopher Marlowe
Doctor Faustus

Arthur Miller
Death of a Salesman

Toni Morrison
Beloved

William Shakespeare
Antony and Cleopatra

William Shakespeare
As You Like It

William Shakespeare
Hamlet

William Shakespeare
King Lear

William Shakespeare
Measure for Measure

William Shakespeare
The Merchant of Venice

William Shakespeare
Much Ado About Nothing

William Shakespeare
Othello

William Shakespeare
Romeo and Juliet

William Shakespeare
The Tempest

William Shakespeare
The Winter's Tale

Mary Shelley
Frankenstein

Alice Walker
The Color Purple

Oscar Wilde
The Importance of Being Earnest

Tennessee Williams
A Streetcar Named Desire

John Webster
The Duchess of Malfi

W.B. Yeats
Selected Poems

Chinua Achebe
Things Fall Apart

Edward Albee
Who's Afraid of Virginia Woolf?

Margaret Atwood
Cat's Eye

Jane Austen
Emma

Jane Austen
Northanger Abbey

Jane Austen
Sense and Sensibility

Samuel Beckett
Waiting for Godot

Robert Browning
Selected Poems

Robert Burns
Selected Poems

Angela Carter
Nights at the Circus

Geoffrey Chaucer
The Merchant's Tale

Geoffrey Chaucer
The Miller's Tale

Geoffrey Chaucer
The Nun's Priest's Tale

Samuel Taylor Coleridge
Selected Poems

Daniel Defoe
Moll Flanders

Daniel Defoe
Robinson Crusoe

Charles Dickens
Bleak House

Charles Dickens
Hard Times

Emily Dickinson
Selected Poems

Carol Ann Duffy
Selected Poems

George Eliot
Middlemarch

T.S. Eliot
The Waste Land

T.S. Eliot
Selected Poems

Henry Fielding
Joseph Andrews

E.M. Forster
Howards End

John Fowles
The French Lieutenant's Woman

Robert Frost
Selected Poems

Elizabeth Gaskell
North and South

Stella Gibbons
Cold Comfort Farm

Graham Greene
Brighton Rock

Thomas Hardy
Jude the Obscure

Thomas Hardy
Selected Poems

Joseph Heller
Catch-22

Homer
The Iliad

Homer
The Odyssey

Gerard Manley Hopkins
Selected Poems

Aldous Huxley
Brave New World

Kazuo Ishiguro
The Remains of the Day

Ben Jonson
The Alchemist

Ben Jonson
Volpone

James Joyce
A Portrait of the Artist as a Young Man

Philip Larkin
Selected Poems

D.H. Lawrence
The Rainbow

D.H. Lawrence
Selected Stories

D.H. Lawrence
Sons and Lovers

D.H. Lawrence
Women in Love

John Milton

Paradise Lost Bks I & II

John Milton
Paradise Lost Bks IV & IX

Thomas More
Utopia

Sean O'Casey
Juno and the Paycock

George Orwell
Nineteen Eighty-four

John Osborne
Look Back in Anger

Wilfred Owen
Selected Poems

Sylvia Plath
Selected Poems

Alexander Pope
Rape of the Lock and other poems

Ruth Prawer Jhabvala
Heat and Dust

Jean Rhys
Wide Sargasso Sea

William Shakespeare
As You Like It

William Shakespeare
Coriolanus

William Shakespeare
Henry IV Pt 1

William Shakespeare
Henry V

William Shakespeare
Julius Caesar

William Shakespeare
Macbeth

William Shakespeare
Measure for Measure

William Shakespeare
A Midsummer Night's Dream

William Shakespeare
Richard II

William Shakespeare
Richard III

William Shakespeare
Sonnets

William Shakespeare
The Taming of the Shrew

William Shakespeare
Richard III

William Shakespeare
Sonnets

William Shakespeare
The Taming of the Shrew

William Shakespeare
Twelfth Night

William Shakespeare
The Winter's Tale

George Bernard Shaw
Arms and the Man

George Bernard Shaw
Saint Joan

Muriel Spark
The Prime of Miss Jean Brodie

John Steinbeck
The Grapes of Wrath

John Steinbeck
The Pearl

Tom Stoppard
Arcadia

Tom Stoppard
Rosencrantz and Guildenstern are Dead

Jonathan Swift
Gulliver's Travels and The Modest Proposal

Alfred, Lord Tennyson
Selected Poems

W.M. Thackeray
Vanity Fair

Virgil
The Aeneid

Edith Wharton
The Age of Innocence

Tennessee Williams
Cat on a Hot Tin Roof

Tennessee Williams
The Glass Menagerie

Virginia Woolf
Mrs Dalloway

Virginia Woolf
To the Lighthouse

William Wordsworth
Selected Poems

Metaphysical Poets

York Notes – the Ultimate Literature Guides

York Notes are recognised as the best literature study guides. If you have enjoyed using this book and have found it useful, you can now order others directly from us – simply follow the ordering instructions below.

HOW TO ORDER

Decide which title(s) you require and then order in one of the following ways:

Booksellers
All titles available from good bookstores.

By post
List the title(s) you require in the space provided overleaf, select your method of payment, complete your name and address details and return your completed order form and payment to:

Addison Wesley Longman Ltd
PO BOX 88
Harlow
Essex CM19 5SR

By phone
Call our Customer Information Centre on 01279 623923 to place your order, quoting mail number: HEYN1.

By fax
Complete the order form overleaf, ensuring you fill in your name and address details and method of payment, and fax it to us on 01279 414130.

By e-mail
E-mail your order to us on awlhe.orders@awl.co.uk listing title(s) and quantity required and providing full name and address details as requested overleaf. Please quote mail number: HEYN1. Please do not send credit card details by e-mail.

York Notes Order Form

Titles required:

Quantity	Title/ISBN	Price

Sub total _____

Please add £2.50 postage & packing _____

(*P & P is free for orders over £50*) _____

Total _____

Mail no: HEYN1

Your Name _____

Your Address _____
_____

Postcode _____ Telephone _____

Method of payment

☐ I enclose a cheque or a P/O for £_____ made payable to Addison Wesley Longman Ltd

☐ Please charge my Visa/Access/AMEX/Diners Club card
Number _____ Expiry Date _____
Signature _____ Date _____

(please ensure that the address given above is the same as for your credit card)

Prices and other details are correct at time of going to press but may change without notice. All orders are subject to status.

☐ *Please tick this box if you would like a complete listing of Longman Study Guides (suitable for GCSE and A-level students)*

York Press

Longman

Addison Wesley Longman